Francis Frith's
THE PEAK DISTRICT

PHOTOGRAPHIC MEMORIES

Francis Frith's
THE PEAK DISTRICT

◆

Roly Smith

FRITH
BOOK Co

First published in the United Kingdom in 2000 by
Frith Book Company Ltd

Hardback Edition 2000
ISBN 1-85937-100-0

Paperback Edition 2001
ISBN 1-85937-280-5

Hardback Reprinted 2001

British Library Cataloguing in Publication Data

Francis Frith's The Peak District
Roly Smith

Frith Book Company Ltd
Frith's Barn, Teffont,
Salisbury, Wiltshire SP3 5QP
Tel: +44 (0) 1722 716 376
Email: info@frithbook.co.uk
www.frithbook.co.uk

Printed and bound in Great Britain

AS WITH ANY HISTORICAL DATABASE THE FRITH ARCHIVE IS CONSTANTLY BEING CORRECTED AND IMPROVED
AND THE PUBLISHERS WOULD WELCOME INFORMATION ON OMISSIONS OR INACCURACIES

Contents

Francis Frith: Victorian Pioneer   7

Frith's Archive - A Unique Legacy   10

The Peak District - An Introduction   12

The Southern Peak   16

The Central Peak   26

The Hope Valley   56

The Derwent Valley   70

The North & West Peak   88

Index   115

Free Mounted Print Voucher   *119*

FRANCIS FRITH: *Victorian Pioneer*

FRANCIS FRITH, Victorian founder of the world-famous photographic archive, was a complex and fascinating man. A devout Quaker and a highly successful Victorian businessman, he was both philosophic by nature and pioneering in outlook.

By 1855 Francis Frith had already established a wholesale grocery business in Liverpool, and sold it for the astonishing sum of £200,000, which is the equivalent today of over £15,000,000. Now a multi-millionaire, he was able to indulge his passion for travel. As a child he had pored over travel books written by early explorers, and his fancy and imagination had been stirred by family holidays to the sublime mountain regions of Wales and Scotland. 'What a land of spirit-stirring and enriching scenes and places!' he had written. He was to return to these scenes of grandeur in later years to 'recapture the thousands of vivid and tender memories', but with a different purpose. Now in his thirties, and captivated by the new science of photography, Frith set out on a series of pioneering journeys to the Nile regions that occupied him from 1856 until 1860.

INTRIGUE AND ADVENTURE

He took with him on his travels a specially-designed wicker carriage that acted as both dark-room and sleeping chamber. These far-flung journeys were packed with intrigue and adventure. In his life story, written when he was sixty-three, Frith tells of being held captive by bandits, and of fighting 'an awful midnight battle to the very point of surrender with a deadly pack of hungry, wild dogs'. Sporting flowing Arab costume, Frith arrived at Akaba by camel seventy years before Lawrence, where he encountered 'desert princes and rival sheikhs, blazing with jewel-hilted swords'.

During these extraordinary adventures he was assiduously exploring the desert regions bordering the Nile and patiently recording the antiquities and peoples with his camera. He was the first photographer to venture beyond the sixth cataract. Africa was still the mysterious 'Dark Continent', and Stanley and Livingstone's historic meeting was a decade into the future. The conditions for picture taking confound belief. He laboured for hours in his wicker dark-room in the sweltering heat of the desert, while the volatile chemicals fizzed dangerously in their trays. Often he was forced to work in remote tombs and caves where conditions were cooler. Back in London he exhibited his photographs and was 'rapturously cheered' by members of the Royal Society. His reputation as a photographer was made overnight. An eminent modern historian has likened their impact on the population of the time to that on our own generation of the first photographs taken on the surface of the moon.

VENTURE OF A LIFE-TIME

Characteristically, Frith quickly spotted the opportunity to create a new business as a specialist publisher of photographs. He lived in an era of immense and sometimes violent change. For the poor in the early part of Victoria's reign work was a drudge and the hours long, and people had precious little free time to enjoy themselves.

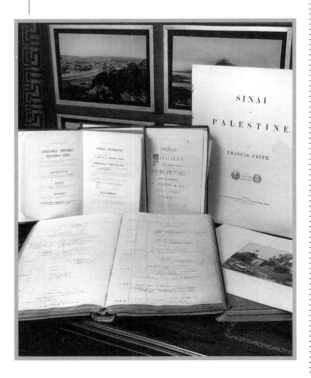

Most had no transport other than a cart or gig at their disposal, and had not travelled far beyond the boundaries of their own town or village. However, by the 1870s, the railways had threaded their way across the country, and Bank Holidays and half-day Saturdays had been made obligatory by Act of Parliament. All of a sudden the ordinary working man and his family were able to enjoy days out and see a little more of the world.

With characteristic business acumen, Francis Frith foresaw that these new tourists would enjoy having souvenirs to commemorate their days out. In 1860 he married Mary Ann Rosling and set out with the intention of photographing every city, town and village in Britain. For the next thirty years he travelled the country by train and by pony and trap, producing fine photographs of seaside resorts and beauty spots that were keenly bought by millions of Victorians. These prints were painstakingly pasted into family albums and pored over during the dark nights of winter, rekindling precious memories of summer excursions.

THE RISE OF FRITH & CO

Frith's studio was soon supplying retail shops all over the country. To meet the demand he gathered about him a small team of photographers, and published the work of independent artist-photographers of the calibre of Roger Fenton and Francis Bedford. In order to gain some understanding of the scale of Frith's business one only has to look at the catalogue issued by Frith & Co in 1886: it runs to some 670

pages, listing not only many thousands of views of the British Isles but also many photographs of most European countries, and China, Japan, the USA and Canada – note the sample page shown above from the hand-written *Frith & Co* ledgers detailing pictures taken. By 1890 Frith had created the greatest specialist photographic publishing company in the world, with over 2,000 outlets – more than the combined number that Boots and WH Smith have today! The picture on the right shows the *Frith & Co* display board at Ingleton in the Yorkshire Dales. Beautifully constructed with mahogany frame and gilt inserts, it could display up to a dozen local scenes.

POSTCARD BONANZA

The ever-popular holiday postcard we know today took many years to develop. In 1870 the Post Office issued the first plain cards, with a pre-printed stamp on one face. In 1894 they allowed other publishers' cards to be sent through the mail with an attached adhesive halfpenny stamp. Demand grew rapidly, and in 1895 a new size of postcard was permitted called the

court card, but there was little room for illustration. In 1899, a year after Frith's death, a new card measuring 5.5 x 3.5 inches became the standard format, but it was not until 1902 that the divided back came into being, with address and message on one face and a full-size illustration on the other. *Frith & Co* were in the vanguard of postcard development, and Frith's sons Eustace and Cyril continued their father's monumental task, expanding the number of views offered to the public and recording more and more places in Britain, as the coasts and countryside were opened up to mass travel.

Francis Frith died in 1898 at his villa in Cannes, his great project still growing. The archive he created continued in business for another seventy years. By 1970 it contained over a third of a million pictures of 7,000 cities, towns and villages. The massive photographic record Frith has left to us stands as a living monument to a special and very remarkable man.

Frith's Archive: *A Unique Legacy*

FRANCIS FRITH'S legacy to us today is of immense significance and value, for the magnificent archive of evocative photographs he created provides a unique record of change in 7,000 cities, towns and villages throughout Britain over a century and more. Frith and his fellow studio photographers revisited locations many times down the years to update their views, compiling for us an enthralling and colourful pageant of British life and character.

We tend to think of Frith's sepia views of Britain as nostalgic, for most of us use them to conjure up memories of places in our own lives with which we have family associations. It often makes us forget that to Francis Frith they were records of daily life as it was actually being lived in the cities, towns and villages of his day. The Victorian age was one of great and often bewildering change for ordinary people, and though the pictures evoke an impression of slower times, life was as busy and hectic as it is today.

We are fortunate that Frith was a photographer of the people, dedicated to recording the minutiae of everyday life. For it is this sheer wealth of visual data, the painstaking chronicle of changes in dress, transport, street layouts, buildings, housing, engineering and landscape that captivates us so much today. His remarkable images offer us a powerful link with the past and with the lives of our ancestors.

TODAY'S TECHNOLOGY

Computers have now made it possible for Frith's many thousands of images to be accessed almost instantly. In the Frith archive today, each photograph is carefully 'digitised' then stored on a CD Rom. Frith archivists can locate a single photograph amongst thousands within seconds. Views can be catalogued and sorted under a variety of categories of place and content to the immediate benefit of researchers. Inexpensive reference prints can be created for them at the touch of a mouse button, and a wide range of books and other printed materials assembled and published for a wider, more general readership - in the next twelve months over a hundred Frith local history titles will be published! The

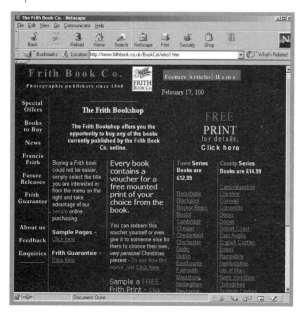

See Frith at www. frithbook.co.uk

day-to-day workings of the archive are very different from how they were in Francis Frith's time: imagine the herculean task of sorting through eleven tons of glass negatives as Frith had to do to locate a particular sequence of pictures! Yet the archive still prides itself on maintaining the same high standards of excellence laid down by Francis Frith, including the painstaking cataloguing and indexing of every view.

It is curious to reflect on how the internet now allows researchers in America and elsewhere greater instant access to the archive than Frith himself ever enjoyed. Many thousands of individual views can be called up on screen within seconds on one of the Frith internet sites, enabling people living continents away to revisit the streets of their ancestral home town, or view places in Britain where they have enjoyed holidays. Many overseas researchers welcome the chance to view special theme selections, such as transport, sports, costume and ancient monuments.

We are certain that Francis Frith would have heartily approved of these modern developments, for he himself was always working at the very limits of Victorian photographic technology.

THE VALUE OF THE ARCHIVE TODAY

Because of the benefits brought by the computer, Frith's images are increasingly studied by social historians, by researchers into genealogy and ancestory, by architects, town planners, and by teachers and schoolchildren involved in local history projects. In addition, the archive offers every one of

us a unique opportunity to examine the places where we and our families have lived and worked down the years. Immensely successful in Frith's own era, the archive is now, a century and more on, entering a new phase of popularity.

THE PAST IN TUNE WITH THE FUTURE

Historians consider the Francis Frith Collection to be of prime national importance. It is the only archive of its kind remaining in private ownership and has been valued at a million pounds. However, this figure is now rapidly increasing as digital technology enables more and more people around the world to enjoy its benefits.

Francis Frith's archive is now housed in an historic timber barn in the beautiful village of Teffont in Wiltshire. Its founder would not recognize the archive office as it is today. In place of the many thousands of dusty boxes containing glass plate negatives and an all-pervading odour of photographic chemicals, there are now ranks of computer screens. He would be amazed to watch his images travelling round the world at unimaginable speeds through network and internet lines.

The archive's future is both bright and exciting. Francis Frith, with his unshakeable belief in making photographs available to the greatest number of people, would undoubtedly approve of what is being done today with his lifetime's work. His photographs, depicting our shared past, are now bringing pleasure and enlightenment to millions around the world a century and more after his death.

THE PEAK DISTRICT – *An Introduction*

THE PEAK DISTRICT, the last vertebra in the stony backbone of England, is an area full of paradoxes. Despite the name, there are few hills which really justify the name 'peak'. The name originates from the Old English peac which meant a knoll or hill, and did not have the modern dictionary meaning of 'a sharply pointed summit'. The most common perspective in the Peak is, in fact, that of horizontal plateaux.

Another Peak District paradox is the name 'low', so common on Peak District maps. There are 70 of these on the limestone White Peak plateau alone, and almost without exception, they mark a hill or a high point in the landscape. The confusing name also comes from an Old English word - hlaw - which meant a burial mound or hill, and usually denotes a tumulus dating from the Bronze Age. So where you see 'low' in the Peak District, it usually denotes a high place.

History shows us that the Peak has always been a place set apart from the rest of Britain. Its earliest-known named inhabitants were the Saxon tribe known as the Pecsaetan - the 'people of the Peak' - a separate and independent tribe from the Mercians who ruled much of central England during the Dark Ages. This apartness is echoed in the many strange and often unique ancient customs and legends which have lived on in the limestone and grit-stone hills of the Peak, long after they have disappeared elsewhere in Britain. Examples of these which are still practised are the ancient, originally pagan, custom of well-dressing, and the mysterious Castleton Garlanding Ceremony, which was perhaps instituted as a pagan celebration of the return of spring.

DARK AND WHITE

There are two, quite distinct types of scenery in the Peak District - imparting contrasting, almost male and female, characteristics to the landscape. These very different landscapes have been given the names Dark Peak and White Peak, and have been widely adopted now, even on Ordnance Survey maps. The physical relationship between the Dark Peak and White Peak is perhaps best described by imagining a man's balding head. The remaining 'hair' can be seen as the Dark Peak moors to the north, east and west, leaving the 'skin' of the central limestone plateau of the White Peak exposed in the middle and south.

The Dark Peak is the name given to the northern, eastern and western millstone grit moorlands of the Peak District. This is a macho land of dark, brooding tablelands punctuated by steep, rocky valleys known as cloughs; weird, wind-carved tors or towers of rock; and moorlands bordered by steep walls of naked rock, known as 'edges'. The moors are dominated by heather, bilberry and moor grass, but on the highest points, such as Kinder Scout, Bleaklow and Black Hill, years of over-grazing, acid rain and natural erosion have robbed the soil of vegetation, and left behind only the dark and dank peat bogs. Settlements here are usually isolated villages, sheltering in the dales beneath the moors, although some of the larger towns, like Buxton, Chapel-en-le-Frith and Leek, are also found on the edge of the Dark Peak moors.

Although both the limestone and the millstone grit were formed during the same Carboniferous period about 350 million years ago, the pale limestone of the White Peak is the older of the two rocks. It lies beneath the gritstone moors and edges, but has been exposed by centuries of uplifting and erosion into the 'Derbyshire dome' to create that 'bald patch' which is the 1,000 ft (300m) central limestone plateau, dissected by distinctive, steep-sided dales.

The White Peak is an altogether more gentle, feminine kind of landscape than the Dark Peak. The swelling contours of the limestone plateau are covered by a network of drystone walls; this is the feature of the Peak District which often makes the most lasting impression on first-time visitors, especially those coming from the south. Most of these characteristic walls are about 200 years old, built at the time of the Parliamentary Enclosure Movements of the 18th and 19th centuries, but some have recently been dated to as early as Romano-British times.

The most important prehistoric remains, such as the stone circle and henge of Arbor Low and the Five Wells chambered tomb at

Dovedale, The Stepping Stones 1914 67609

Taddington, for example, are also found high on the limestone plateau, where villages like Tideswell and Monyash shelter in shallow depressions, usually around the village pond or 'mere'.

Most of the White Peak dales are too narrow to accommodate a road, and therefore

Rutland's Haddon Hall, standing on a bluff above the River Wye near Bakewell.

Buxton is by far the biggest town in the Peak District, and where most of its visitors have traditionally stayed. But it only really came to prominence during the 18th century. The 5th Duke of Devonshire used some of the

Buxton, The Crescent 1886 18649

they are almost exclusively the preserve of walkers. Over the years, but especially since the turn of the century, as is shown by the photographs in this collection, they have come in their thousands to enjoy the scenic splendour of places like Dovedale, Monsal Dale and Lathkill Dale.

The broad, well-wooded and fertile shale valleys of the Derwent and the Wye - the Peak's two major rivers - are where many of the Peak District's larger settlements, such as Bakewell and the Matlocks, lie. The shale valleys are also where the local aristocracy built the famous stately homes of the Peak, such as Chatsworth, home of the Duke of Devonshire, on the Derwent near Baslow, and the Duke of

enormous profits he made from his copper and lead mines at Ecton Hill in Staffordshire on a grand building spree which attempted to make Buxton a rival to Bath as a fashionable spa. Buildings like John Carr's splendid Crescent, the Natural Baths and St. Ann's Well serve to remind the visitor of that briefly successful venture, which received its final boost by the coming of the Midland Railway, engineered through the hills of the Peak in 1863.

The tepid spring waters of Buxton also attracted the Romans into the forbidding hills of the Peak District, and they named the town Aqua Arnemetiae. But the chief reason for the Roman expansion into the Peak was the abundant supplies of lead ore in the limestone strata of the White Peak. The Romans were the first to commercially exploit the Peak's lead riches, but the lead mining industry reached its zenith during the 18th and 19th centuries, when almost every White Peak farmer doubled as a lead miner as he operated in a true dual economy.

Bakewell is the unofficial 'capital' of the Peak District, but still has a population of only 4,000 people. With a Saxon foundation, the town has commanded an important crossing of the Wye for well over 1,000 years, and was first awarded a grant for a weekly market in 1254. That market still takes place on a Monday, but no longer in the street in front of the Rutland Arms - birthplace of the traditional delicacy, the Bakewell pudding - but in a controversial new Agricultural and Business Centre on the Bakewell showground across the river.

Another of the major 'honeypots' of the Peak District in these early photographs and today, is Castleton, the township at the head of the Hope Valley. Castleton grew up as a planned settlement in the shadow of William Peveril's castle, lording it on its crag between the gorge of Peak Cavern and Cave Dale. It is probably most famous for its four show caverns, formed at the junction of the limestone with the gritstone, which have attracted visitors since the days of Daniel Defoe and Queen Victoria.

The other stone-built villages in the Peak have hardly changed since Francis Frith first took his camera there at the turn of the 20th century, as many of the following photographs show. Perhaps the greatest change has been in the different forms of transport shown. The horses and carts were gradually superseded by motor vehicles, and children could no longer play in the street as the ancient peace of the dales was shattered by the transport revolution.

FIRST AND LAST

The Peak District became the first National Park in Britain when it was designated in April 1951. It stood out then as the last unspoilt open space between Manchester and Sheffield and the rest of the great conurbations of northern and central England. The populations of those surrounding cities had long used the Peak for their weekend recreation, as is well shown in Frith's earliest photographs. But by the Fifties, the creeping suburbia, roadside signs and the red-brick villas of the fast-expanding cities were insidiously creeping out towards the hills of the Peak, unchecked by any planning restrictions.

The proximity to the huge populations of the Midlands and north - half the population of England lives within 60 miles of the Peak District - has inevitably led to problems of congestion in recent years. It has been claimed that the 22 million day visits to the Peak District National Park make it the second most visited National Park in the world, and the narrow Peakland roads and paths often show signs of serious congestion and wear and tear.

But Frith's unique archive of photographs show us what the Peak District was like before the mass tourism of today took hold. The challenge facing the Peak District National Park Authority today is to continue to safeguard and protect this precious resource so that future generations can continue to enjoy its amazingly unspoilt beauty.

ALSTONEFIELD, MILL DALE C1955 A284002

This is the Lode Mill Bridge over the River Dove in Mill Dale, just below the pleasant Staffordshire village of Alstonefield. The buildings on the left of the photograph, just over the bridge, were established as a lead smelt works, hence the name, and later converted into a corn mill, the wheel of which can still be seen.

ASHBOURNE, THE CHURCH 1886 18570

Novelist George Eliot described the beautiful parish church of St Oswald in Ashbourne as 'the finest mere parish church in England'. Its stately 212ft spire dominates the town, and the fine wrought iron gates seen in the photograph are decorated with skulls and flames and date from around 1700. They were restored with the rest of the church in 1886.

ASHBOURNE, THE GREEN MAN 1886 18577
The Green Man and Black's Head double inn sign in St John Street is a rare example of a 'gallows' sign, extending right across the road. Decorated on one side with the head of a Green Man and on the other by a Turk's head, the signs advertised both these former coaching inns, now combined into one. Note the cobbled street and what appears to be a livery man standing beneath the sign.

ASHBOURNE, MARKET PLACE 1957 A66018
Ashbourne was first recorded as holding a market in 1257, 24 years before the town became a borough, and the triangular, sloping Market Place is still the venue for the weekly event every Saturday. This view looks up the market towards the porticoed Town Hall in the centre of the photograph, and was taken at a time when parking restrictions were apparently unheard of!

BONSALL, THE CROSS C1955 B485013

Bonsall's 17th-century Market Cross is set into the hillside of its steeply-sloping Market Square. Bonsall, just off the Via Gellia, was famous as a lead mining village, and the King's Head Inn, to the left in the background of this photograph, dates from 1677 and is said to be haunted. Other pubs include the significantly-named Pig of Lead.

DOVEDALE, GENERAL VIEW 1914 67612

In 1914 the approach to Dovedale, perhaps the most famous of the Peak District dales, could still be accomplished by car, as this photograph shows. Today, the visitor has to park further down the dale and walk in beneath the slopes of Thorpe Cloud and Buntser Hill to reach the famous Stepping Stones. This track is now well wooded.

DOVEDALE, THE STEPPING STONES 1914 67609

This Edwardian family, perhaps the same one which was in the car in picture No 67612, step daintily across the Stepping Stones at the entrance to Dovedale. These stones, worn smooth and shiny by generations of visitors, mark the start of the spectacular scenery which has made Dovedale such a popular destination.

DOVEDALE, THORPE CLOUD 1894 34263

DOVEDALE, REYNARD'S CAVE 1914 67603

DOVEDALE
Thorpe Cloud 1894
This photograph of Dovedale's Stepping Stones beneath conical Thorpe Cloud is interesting because it also shows a pair of donkeys in the left foreground: they were used in the early days to take tourists through the dale. Stalls were set up near the Stepping Stones to allow visitors to take advantage of this unusual form of transport.

DOVEDALE
Reynard's Cave 1914
The natural arch of Reynard's Cave is one of the many rock formations which attract tourists to Dovedale. Formed by the differential erosion of the limestone, the cave was the scene of a tragedy in 1761: the Rev Dean Langton attempted to climb the steep slope into the cave on horseback, but his horse slipped and he was killed. The incident is commemorated by a plaque in Ashbourne church.

DOVEDALE, ILAM ROCK 1914 67605

The then ivy-covered fang of Ilam Rock stands clear from the woods on the western (Staffordshire) bank of Dovedale. The path through the dale on the eastern (Derbyshire) bank is now reconstructed and engineered to carry the huge volume of walkers who now annually pass through the dale.

DOVEDALE, DOVEHOLES AND CAPLAIN'S ROCK 1894 34258

The great shallow caves of Doveholes are at the northern end of the famous dale, and were caused by the swirling waters of the Dove as it cut out the dale after the last Ice Age. The upstanding rock to the left of the photograph has had various names bestowed on it, including the Church Rock or Caplains or Captain's Rock.

HARTINGTON, THE CHURCH c1950 H3303104

The parish church of St Giles occupies a commanding position on a hilltop above this pretty village at the northern end of Dovedale. It has a two-storey porch and transepts and aisles dating mainly from the 13th and 14th centuries, while the fine, pinnacled tower is built in the Perpendicular style.

HARTINGTON, THE POND c1950 H3303102

A family pose with their pony by the village pond, locally known as a mere, in the centre of the village. Many White Peak villages owe their existence to the presence of a pond in this fast-draining limestone countryside. The Hartington pond was recently restored and seats were installed by the National Park Authority.

ILAM
The Hall c1965

Ilam Hall was built in a high Gothic, battlemented style by the shipping magnate Jesse Watts Russell in 1828; it was partly demolished in 1934 and became a youth hostel, leased from the National Trust. Watts Russell converted the village in the then-fashionable cottage ornée style, with houses looking more like Swiss chalets than the solid, Staffordshire vernacular.

◆

MAPPLETON
Okeover Hall c1955

The hamlet of Okeover, north of Ashbourne, is an example of a medieval village which was de-populated to make room for a deer park. The Georgian red-brick mansion, on the left of the photograph, was a later addition, built by the Okeover family in 1780, but the medieval (14th- to 15th-century) sandstone church is a reminder of that ancient past.

ILAM, THE HALL c1965   D145066

MAPPLETON, OKEOVER HALL c1955   M343024

MAPPLETON, THE VILLAGE c1955 M343027

MAPPLETON
The Village c1955
Mappleton village, standing on the River Dove south of Ashbourne, is probably most famous for the strange, octagonal dome and lantern on its parish church of St Mary. Just to the south of the Peak District proper, Mappleton is very much a village of the Midlands, with red brick houses as opposed to the stone found further north.

THORPE
The Church 1906
The Parish Church of St Leonard at Thorpe has a squat Norman tower and many other features of interest. Thorpe's Norse name - it means an outlying farm or hamlet - gives away its ancient origins, but today it is probably best-known as the gateway village to Dovedale, with the reef limestone peak of Thorpe Cloud ('cloud' is Old English for rock or hill) standing guard at the southern entrance.

THORPE, THE CHURCH 1906 53436

WIRKSWORTH, GENERAL VIEW c1960 W351007

The old mining town of Wirksworth was founded on the wealth won from lead and limestone. Surrounded by huge limestone quarries and the remains of thousands of old lead mines, Wirksworth retains its links with the lead industry in the shape of its Moot Hall in Chapel Lane, where the lead miners' Barmoor Court still meets twice a year to settle disputes.

WIRKSWORTH, ST MARY'S CHURCH c1960 W351004

Standing in a close almost like a cathedral, St Mary's Church at Wirksworth dates mainly from the 13th and 14th centuries, but was heavily restored in 1876. Among its many treasures is an intricately carved 7th-century Saxon coffin lid, featuring stories from the life of Christ. There is also a famous little carving of a medieval lead miner, 't'owd man', indicating the source of the town's wealth.

ALPORT, MILL BRIDGE C1960 A333024
The pretty little limestone village of Alport, just off the Bakewell-Youlgreave road, stands at the confluence of the Lathkill and Bradford rivers. The Mill Bridge is a graceful, 18th-century structure at the entrance to the village, near to the site of the former corn mill.

ASHFORD-IN-THE-WATER, HOLY TRINITY CHURCH C1955 A324020
Ashford's parish church of the Holy Trinity stands in the centre of the village. It was heavily restored in 1870, but it retains the base of its 13th-century tower and a Norman tympanum over the south door. Inside are some fine examples of Ashford's most famous product, the polished limestone known as Ashford Black Marble, which was very fashionable in Victorian times.

ASHFORD-IN-THE-WATER, THE DAY'S WORK DONE C1955 A324001
By the mid-Fifties, heavy horses were still in use on many Peak District farms; the ubiquitous tractor had still to take over. The horseman gives his horse a well-earned drink at the end of the day from the shallows in the River Wye near Ashford's famous Sheepwash Bridge, where sheep are still tossed into the river to clean their fleeces before shearing.

ASHFORD-IN-THE-WATER, OLD COTTAGES c1955 A324002
A young girl and her sister push their toy pram past an ancient, ivy-covered limestone cottage with mullioned windows and a quaint, cobbled yard adjacent to a farm barn. This is a scene which had hardly changed in a hundred years in many Peakland villages.

ASHFORD-IN-THE-WATER, THE TOP PUMP c1955 A324017
The Top Pump, at the junction of what was once the main Bakewell-Buxton road and the minor road to Monsal Dale, is the scene of one of Ashford's famous well dressings, held annually in early June. These beautiful floral icons are unique to the Peak District, and Ashford decorates six different wells or springs.

BAKEWELL
General View 1894

This view of Bakewell's Parish Church of All Saints from Yeld Road has hardly changed in over a century. There has been a little infilling of houses in the foreground, but the view of the Peak District's major market town remains essentially the same today. The church had been extensively rebuilt some 40 years before this photograph was taken.

◆

BAKEWELL
Rutland Square 1914

The elegant Georgian coaching inn known as the Rutland Arms, with the parish church on the hill behind, dominate this almost completely traffic-free view of the centre of Bakewell. Dogs could roam freely in what is now a very busy road junction on the A6 trunk road between Derby and Manchester.

BAKEWELL, GENERAL VIEW 1894 34252

BAKEWELL, RUTLAND SQUARE 1914 67616

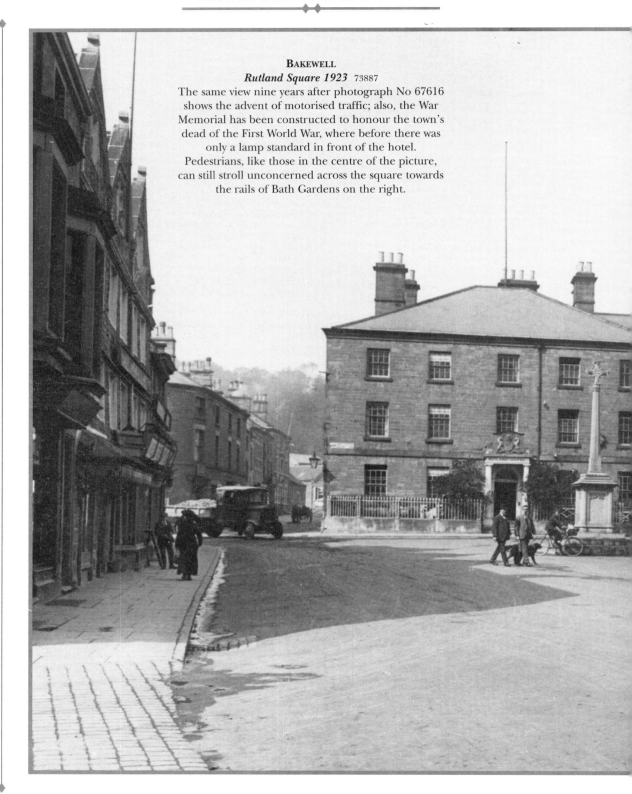

BAKEWELL
Rutland Square 1923 73887
The same view nine years after photograph No 67616
shows the advent of motorised traffic; also, the War
Memorial has been constructed to honour the town's
dead of the First World War, where before there was
only a lamp standard in front of the hotel.
Pedestrians, like those in the centre of the picture,
can still stroll unconcerned across the square towards
the rails of Bath Gardens on the right.

BAKEWELL
Rutland Square 1923 73889
A closer view of the war memorial is seen in this view taken looking down
the Square towards the river from the Rutland Arms. Deacon's Bank, now
the Royal Bank of Scotland, is on the left, while Orme's department store
is on the extreme right, next to Stewart's Clothing Hall. Interestingly, this
part of Bakewell is still known as Orme's Corner to older local people.

BAKEWELL, THE OLD ORIGINAL BAKEWELL PUDDING SHOP c1965 B6100

This late 17th-century shop in Bridge Street started life as a chandler's shop making candles, but the wife of the chandler was the first to see the commercial possibilities of the Bakewell Pudding. She obtained the recipe from the cook at the Rutland Arms, who had 'invented' the delicacy by mistake in the 1860s.

BAKEWELL, OLD COTTAGES 1914 67617

At this time, the central cottage in this row in South Church Street was still thatched, probably with heather from the surrounding moors. Apart from the roofing material and the ivy-clad walls, the cottages have not changed much today, and the spire of the church still watches over in the background.

BAKEWELL, THE BRIDGE 1894 34254

Bakewell's superb five-arched bridge dates from the 14th century, and is one of the oldest in the country still in use by heavy traffic. The downstream (southern) side of the bridge was rebuilt when the road was widened, but essentially the same structure has been in use for well over 600 years.

BAKEWELL, OLD PACK HORSE BRIDGE 1923 73896

Just upstream from the town's main bridge is this narrow packhorse bridge, known as Holme Bridge; it was rebuilt in 1664 to take the long trains of packhorses laden with lead and other products across the river towards Chesterfield and the east. The low parapets were deliberately designed so as not to obstruct the panniers hanging from the horses' flanks.

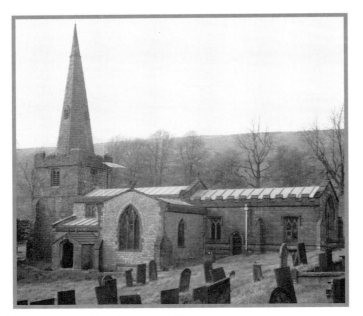

CHELMORTON, THE CHURCH c1960 C401004

CHELMORTON
The Church c1960

The Parish Church of St John the Baptist is built into the side of Chelmorton Low, the tumuli-topped hill which overlooks the village. The elegant 15th-century spire, topped by a weathervane in the form of a locust in honour of the patron saint, is recessed onto a 13th-century tower.

CHELMORTON
The Village c1960

Chelmorton is one of the highest villages in England, standing at well over 1,000ft (300m). In the centre of this view of the village is the unusual stone-built telephone box, next to the school road sign. The stream which runs down by the side of the village street has the charming name of Illy Willy Water.

CHELMORTON, THE VILLAGE c1960 C401009

EDENSOR, THE VILLAGE c1960 E130006

The elegant spire of Sir George Gilbert Scott's Parish Church of St Peter at Edensor, the village in the grounds of Chatsworth Park, dominates this view. The entire village was constructed to the design of the 6th Duke of Devonshire in 1839 because the existing medieval village apparently spoiled the view from the great house.

EYAM, THE VILLAGE 1896 37812

This general view of the main village street could not have changed much since the days of the famous 'visitation' of the plague in 1665/66. Local people stand in front of a horse and cart and curiously eye the photographer as he takes his shot. Filling the background is Eyam Edge, while the inn on the left advertises 'good stabling'.

EYAM, THE PLAGUE COTTAGES 1910 69211
The gabled cottages in front of the church is where the dreaded outbreak of the plague first broke out in Eyam in 1665. Eventually, after the villagers had imposed their own quarantine to stop the disease spreading, over 350 were dead, including the wife of their leader, the vicar, the Rev William Mompesson. The bonneted Edwardian dress of the children posing by the wall is interesting to note.

GREAT LONGSTONE, GENERAL VIEW 1919 69206

A general view of the village of Great Longstone, two miles north of Bakewell, shows the gentle, rolling and well-wooded nature of the countryside in this part of the Peak District. Longstone is situated under the prominent limestone ridge of Longstone Edge, which has been mined for lead and more recently fluorspar for many centuries.

GREAT LONGSTONE, THE VILLAGE c1950 G181004

The main village street of Great Longstone still has the wide, grassy verge seen in this photograph, and the war memorial, just seen beneath the trees in the centre of the photograph, still stands near the entrance to the village school, which is off to the right. The village cross is on the extreme right.

GREAT LONGSTONE, THE CROSS c1950 G181307B

The ancient sandstone cross on the linear village green in Great Longstone has stood watch over the affairs of the village since medieval times. The name of the nearby public house, the Crispin, gives a clue to one of the village's important former industries, for St Crispin is the patron saint of boot and shoe makers.

HADDON HALL 1896 37867

This unusual view of Haddon Hall, family seat of the Dukes of Rutland and one of the finest medieval manor houses in England, was taken downstream from the main entrance, across the River Wye. It shows how the house was originally built on a limestone bluff overlooking the river. We can see the oldest part of the house, the Chapel, which was built in the 14th century.

HADDON HALL, THE ENTRANCE TOWER 1886 18630
Frock-coated and top-hatted Victorians pose for the camera while on an excursion outside the North West Gate or Entrance Tower to Haddon Hall. The tower dates from the 15th century; it was built by Sir Henry Vernon along with the other buildings along the west front, the dining room and Great Chamber.

HADDON HALL, THE TERRACE WALK 1902 48189
These massive, overpowering yew trees which covered the Upper Terrace of the Haddon Gardens were felled shortly after this photograph was taken, and replaced with more manageable trees. The 9th Duke and Duchess of Rutland were responsible for the restoration of the gardens to their present, much admired condition.

HADDON HALL, THE STATE BED 1902 48192
The great State Bed of Haddon, seen here, was removed from the State Bedroom during the restoration of the house begun by the 9th Duke in 1920. It is now kept in the Picture Gallery at the Duke of Rutland's other family seat at Belvoir Castle in Rutland. The unusual 16th-century plaster relief above the fireplace depicts Orpheus charming the beasts.

MILLER'S DALE, THE VILLAGE 1914 67598
The tiny village of Miller's Dale was put on the map in the 1860s by the Midland Railway, for which it was the junction for the spa town of Buxton. The River Wye passes through a deep gorge here, passing the Victorian Gothic parish church of St Anne, built in 1880 by Canon Samuel Andrew of nearby Tideswell.

MILLER'S DALE, GENERAL VIEW 1894 34240
Seen from across the River Wye, the quarry seen on the skyline at Miller's Dale provided limestone for the limekilns alongside the Midland Railway line, which emptied their products straight into railway wagons for transportation. The quarry is now a local nature reserve for the Derbyshire Wildlife Trust.

MONSAL DALE
The Viaduct 1914 67588
A north-bound steam train thunders across the Monsal Dale viaduct, with the escarpment of Fin Cop towering above the River Wye to the left in the background. It was the construction of this railway line in the 1860s which famously excited the wrath of John Ruskin, who deplored the loss of the peace and tranquillity of the valley.

MONSAL DALE, GENERAL VIEW C1955 M221066

A general view of Upper Dale, Monsal Dale. Above the hamlet, the Midland line enters the Brushfield tunnel, one of many on the expensive section of line between Bakewell and Buxton which now forms the Monsal Trail. There are long-term plans to re-open the line for passenger and freight traffic.

MONSAL DALE, THE MONSAL HEAD HOTEL C1955 M221016

The Monsal Head Hotel, with its incongruous Tyrolean balcony, has been a landmark above the famous dale of the River Wye for many years. It commands a wonderful view down the dale, across the famous Monsal Dale viaduct, and north towards Upper Dale.

OVER HADDON, LATHKILL DALE 1914 67625
Framed by an elegant ash tree, the weirs of the River Lathkill in Lathkill Dale seen here were constructed to encourage fish, particularly trout, to breed and spawn. Lathkill Dale, once the scene of lead mining, is now part of the Derbyshire Dales National Nature Reserve, and a haven for wildlife of all sorts.

OVER HADDON, CONKSBURY BRIDGE c1960 O77003
Low-arched Conksbury Bridge, on the back road between Bakewell and Youlgreave, is a medieval construction, first mentioned in 1269 and dating from the time that there was a thriving village here at the lower end of Lathkill Dale. The village, mentioned in the Domesday Book, was later totally deserted, and nothing remains to be seen today.

STONEY MIDDLETON, THE CHURCH C1960 S452025
St Martin's Parish Church is one of the most unusual in the Peak District. Although the tower dates from the 15th century, the body of the church is octagonal with a lantern roof on piers, and dates from a thorough reconstruction of 1759. The church is hidden away in a close off the main street.

STONEY MIDDLETON, MAIN STREET 1951 M122001
Although the caption to this photograph claims this to be Stoney Middleton's Main Street, in fact it is one of the many side streets which branch off the busy main road between Chesterfield and Chapel-en-le-Frith. The solidly-built limestone cottages are typical of this working village, which has many active limestone quarries at its western end.

STONEY MIDDLETON, LOVER'S LEAP 1896 37820
The towering limestone cliffs of Lover's Leap mark the entrance to Middleton Dale at Stoney Middleton. The feature gets its name from a local girl, Hannah Badderley, who after being jilted by her lover, decided to kill herself by leaping from the cliff high above the village street. She was thwarted, however, by her voluminous petticoats, which acted like a parachute and saved her life.

STONEY MIDDLETON, LOOKING WEST 1896 37821
These fine cliffs at the western end of Middleton Dale have become a favourite haunt of rock climbers, with airy routes such as Windhover and Aurora on their vertical buttresses. When this photograph was taken, however, climbers would not venture onto such risky rock. This view would not be possible today, because of subsequent tree growth in the dale.

STONEY MIDDLETON, SHINY CLIFF 1896 37824
This fine buttress at the junction of the road to Eyam is now known as Shining Cliff. Note the peacefully grazing horse on the grassy island in the foreground, and the quaint farmyard scene beneath the cliff. Today, the scene is far from peaceful, with a constant stream of quarry lorries and other traffic on the A623 Chesterfield-Chapel road.

STONEY MIDDLETON, THE DELPH 1896 37825
The Delph leads up from Middleton Dale towards the village of Eyam. At its head is Cucklett Delph, a rocky outcrop where the Rev William Mompesson conducted open-air services during the visitation of the plague to Eyam in 1665-66, and where an annual commemorative service is still held.

TIDESWELL, QUEEN STREET c1960 T46001
Traffic is notable by its absence in this view of Queen Street. The War Memorial is prominent in the centre of the photograph, and the pinnacles of the tower of the parish church peep over the houses in the background.

TIDESWELL, MARKET SQUARE c1960 T46005
Another peaceful high summer view of the prosperous White Peak village. Tideswell's wealth was founded on the dual economies of lead and sheep farming; its magnificent parish Church of St John the Baptist is the finest in the Peak, and known with some justification as 'the Cathedral of the Peak'.

WINSTER, THE MARKET HOUSE c1955 W569001

The Old Market Hall at Winster dates from the late 17th century; it was the first property to be acquired by the National Trust in the Peak District in 1906. An antique show was being advertised as taking place there in this mid-1950s photograph. The Market Hall originally had open arches to its ground floor, like that at Bakewell.

WINSTER, MAIN STREET c1955 W569003

Winster is one of the Peak District's most perfect 18th-century villages; it has a wealth of fine Georgian buildings, such as Winster Hall, whose entrance gates can be seen below the trees in the centre right of this photograph.

WINSTER, WEST BANK c1955 W569009

West Bank winds up the hill towards the significantly-named Miners' Standard public house on the hill above the village. The 'standard' related to the standard measuring dish for lead, for Winster in its heyday was yet another lead mining village, and almost every family had someone employed in the industry.

WINSTER, ROBIN HOOD'S STRIDE c1955 Y14021

The weird gritstone outcrop of Robin Hood's Stride, near Winster, used to have the alternative name of Mock Beggar's Hall, because of its resemblance to a ruined building. The twin pinnacles, known as the Weasel Pinnacle and the Inaccessible Pinnacle, are about 66 feet apart, so Robin Hood must have been a giant!

YOULGREAVE
The Church c1955

The splendid Perpendicular tower of Youlgreave's parish church of All Saints is one of the best in the Peak District, and commands every view of the long main street of this busy village above Bradford Dale. Locally nicknamed 'Pommy', Youlgreave has had over 60 different spellings of its name over the years, but locals prefer 'Youlgrave'.

◆

YOULGREAVE
The Old Coach Road c1955

The Old Coach Road winds through Bradford Dale below Youlgreave, and was the old route into the village from Bakewell and Alport. Today, the 'road' is a pleasant footpath, passing beneath the beetling cliffs of limestone known as Rhienstor with the River Bradford and the bridge to Alport on the left of the photograph.

YOULGREAVE, THE CHURCH c1955 Y14023

YOULGREAVE, THE OLD COACH ROAD c1955 Y14009

BRADWELL, THE VILLAGE 1919 69174
The Hope Valley village of Bradwell has not changed materially since this photograph was taken. It shows the grey, limestone cottages of the former lead mining village beneath the escarpment of Bradwell Edge in the background. The disturbed ground in the centre and right of the photograph is probably the site of former lead mine workings.

BRADWELL, THE VILLAGE c1955 B486011
This view of Bradwell down the steep slope of Smithy Lane also has Bradwell Edge as a backdrop. Note the non-conformist chapel on the right of the photograph, a common feature in most Peak District villages, and a centre for village worship.

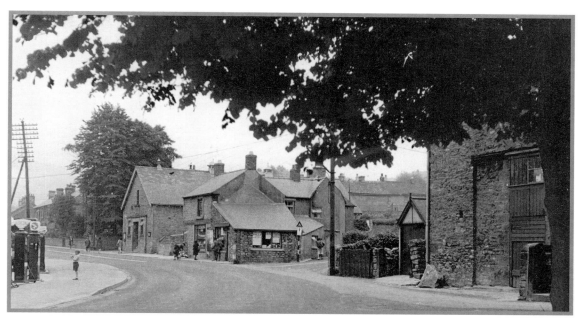

BRADWELL, TOWN END C1955 B486001

Many Peak District villages, however small, have a Town End or Head, and Bradwell is no exception. In medieval days, even small villages were called 'towns'; the neighbouring villages of Flagg and Chelmorton provide other local examples. The traffic-free scene shown here is a reminder of quieter days.

BRADWELL, BROOKSIDE C1955 B486014

Bradwell Brook, seen here, was once the source of power for several mills in Bradwell, although none exist today until the stream reaches Brough and its confluence with the River Noe. Bradwell was famous for its 'Bradder beaver' hats, which were used by lead miners.

BRADWELL, ST IVES C1955 B486015
This area of Bradwell, where the bridge crosses the Bradwell Brook, was known as St Ives when this photograph
was taken. The building on the right close to the stream was probably one of Bradwell's former mills. Note the old-
fashioned telephone box just over the bridge.

BRADWELL, THE CHURCH c1955 B486018

Bradwell's restored parish church stands at the southern end of the village. This is known as Dale End; it enters the steep-sided Bradwell Dale, where there are several reminders of former lead mining activities in the steep limestone walls. Bagshaw Cavern, up the hill opposite the church, was discovered by lead miners in 1806.

CASTLETON, MARKET PLACE 1909 61776

A stage coach stands ready for its passengers on the extreme right of this photograph of Castleton's Market Place. The barn to the left of the stage coach is now a shop. On the steep hill above the Market Place stands the 11th-century keep of Peveril Castle, behind its ivy-covered curtain wall, the finest medieval monument in the Peak District.

CASTLETON
The Market Place 1909 61777
Here a father and two young children pose awkwardly for the photographer on the vestige of the village green. This view is looking west towards the distant Mam Tor. The fenced tree on the right is now the site of the village's war memorial.

CASTLETON, CROSS STREET 1909 61774

CASTLETON
Cross Street 1909

A view of the main shopping street shows the Nag's Head Hotel at the end of the houses on the right, and a huge advertising hoarding nearer to the camera, advising tourists - 'Do Not Fail to See the Blue John Caverns'. Castleton's famous show caves were obviously its fortune even then.

CASTLETON
How Lane 1919

How Lane is the main approach road to Castleton from Sheffield and the east, and is lined with hotels and inns such as Ye Olde Cheshire Cheese (proprietor Lucy Phoenix, and advertising garage and stabling) on the left, and the Peak Hotel further down the street.

CASTLETON, HOW LANE 1919 69169

CASTLETON, THE RIVER STYX 1909 61778
The River Styx was the fanciful Victorian name given to Peakshole Water, which flows out from the awesome entrance to Peak Cavern, the largest in Britain, at Castleton. The walled path on the right leads up to Peak Cavern, which was anciently known as The Devil's Arse, hence the name of the river running through Hell which issues from it.

CASTLETON, SPEEDWELL CAVERN 1909 61785
This charming view of the entrance to Speedwell Cavern at the foot of The Winnats Pass shows how little traffic used the road at the time. The shepherd with his flock and dog stand at the entrance to the dramatic limestone gorge, while Edwardian visitors wait to go down the underground canal to reach Speedwell's 'Bottomless Pit'.

GREAT HUCKLOW, THE EDGE c1960   G180025

GREAT HUCKLOW
The Edge c1960
The former lead mining village of Great Hucklow is situated under the steep escarpment of Hucklow Edge, seen in the background of this photograph. Some remains of former lead mining activity can be seen to the left. At this time, Hucklow was well-known for its outstanding amateur dramatic group known as the Hucklow Players.

◆

GREAT HUCKLOW
Hope Valley and Bradwell c1960
This sweeping view from the Tideswell-Bradwell road shows the heights of Hucklow Edge to the right, the bulk of Win Hill in the background, the smoke from the Hope Valley Cement works in the centre, and Lose Hill to the left. The many miles of drystone walls which characterise the White Peak plateau are well shown.

GREAT HUCKLOW, HOPE VALLEY AND BRADWELL c1960   G180043

HATHERSAGE, THE VILLAGE 1902 48914
This view up the Main Street shows the village Post Office on the right and the Ordnance Arms Hotel, with a water tap and weighing-machine on the end wall, on the left. Some ladies of the village chat unconcernedly in the street in their long dresses and large hats.

HATHERSAGE, THE VILLAGE 1902 48917
Taken from almost the same position as photograph No 48914, this view looks in the opposite direction down the Main Street. At the bottom of the street in the centre of the photograph can be seen the chimney, now demolished, of one of Hathersage's needle and pin mills, for which the village was famous.

HATHERSAGE
The George 1919 69193
The George Hotel, at the junction of the Main Street with the road to Grindleford, is still
a major landmark in Hathersage, as it was when this photograph was taken. It is
advertising catering, a bowling green and tea pavilion for the many trippers who came
and still come to the Hope Valley village from Sheffield.

HATHERSAGE, SURPRISE VIEW 1919 69201
This sharp bend on the Ringinglow road into Hathersage is known as the Surprise View because of the extensive vista it commands down the length of the Hope Valley as the traveller drops down off the eastern moors. The early motor car in the photograph is obviously not expecting any traffic coming the other way around the corner!

HATHERSAGE
The Village 1919

The Millstone Inn stands on the minor Surprise View road to Ringinglow out of the village, and takes its name from the once common industry of millstone making in the area. The millstones were carved from the local gritstone edges, where many can still be found abandoned from the time the trade collapsed in the 19th century.

◆

HOPE
The Smithy 1932

At one time, every village had its blacksmith's shop or smithy, to cope with the demands of the mainly horse-drawn transport of the day. This charming scene in the small village of Hope shows the smithy carrying out work on a hay cutter in the middle of the street, while a horse waits patiently on the right to be shod. In the background is the Old Hall Hotel and the sheds of Hope's weekly stock market.

HATHERSAGE, THE VILLAGE 1919 69200

HOPE, THE SMITHY 1932 85261

BAMFORD, THE DERWENT HOTEL 1919 69178
The mock-Tudor façade of 'Ye Derwent Hotel' stands watch over the main street of the village, which lies under Derwent Edge, in the background, and on the road to the Upper Derwent Valley. When this photograph was taken, work was nearing completion on the massive Derwent and Howden dams in the upper part of the valley.

BASLOW, THE BRIDGE c1883 16576
Baslow's elegant 15th-century arched bridge over the River Derwent is situated at the appropriately named Bridge End part of the village. The village wood mill can be seen in the centre of this photograph, with its undershot waterwheel prominent, just above the broad cascade of the weir across the river.

BASLOW, THE VILLAGE c1955 B484006
This is a general view of the Derwentside village. On the right is a lych gate to the parish church of St Anne, which has an unusual clock face bearing the legend VICTORIA 1897 instead of numbers, in celebration of the Queen's jubilee that year. Opposite the church is Coates' grocery and druggist store.

BASLOW, THE HYDROPATHIC ESTABLISHMENT c1884 16582
Although it never rivalled Buxton or Matlock, Baslow's Hydropathic Establishment operated from 1881 to 1936, and later became a hotel before it was demolished. It stood in Bar Road, the old coach road which led out of Baslow across the moors towards Sheffield to the north.

CALVER, THE VILLAGE c1950 C399045

This is actually the area of Calver known as Calver Sough, after an old lead mine and drainage shaft which emerged here. It stands at the crossroads of the Bakewell-Grindleford and Baslow-Stoney Middleton roads, where there are now traffic lights. The petrol station on the right of the picture is now a restaurant, but the Eyre Arms in the centre has not changed.

CALVER, THE CLIFF PARK c1950 C399016

A general view of Calver (pronounced 'Carver') village from the Cliff College Park looking towards Calver Peak, Coombs Dale and Longstone Edge. The scene has changed very little today, although there is a prominent TV mast on Calver Peak now.

CALVER
Cliff College c1950

The Methodist Cliff College, just to the east of Calver village, has a fine reputation for the training of teachers and others in the faith; it occupies a former country house which stands in beautiful grounds beneath Curbar Edge. The facilities are also used for conferences and meetings of all sorts.

CALVER
Cliff College Youth Camp c1950

The Youth Camp at Cliff College offered residential training for young Methodists, and occupied a lovely position below the woods and trees which slope up to the gritstone edge known as Curbar Edge, which takes its name from the neighbouring village of Curbar. There are fine views from here across the Derwent Valley.

CALVER, CLIFF COLLEGE c1950 C399093

CALVER, CLIFF COLLEGE YOUTH CAMP c1950 C399058

CROMFORD, GENERAL VIEW 1892 31290A

This general view of Cromford, taken from Allen's Hill, shows the prominent Greyhound Hotel in the centre of the picture, built by Richard Arkwright as part of his 'model village' plan for workers at his nearby cotton mill. Beyond Greyhound Square, the centre of the village, is Cromford's millpond, known as the Dam.

CROMFORD, WILLERSLEY CASTLE c1955 C193012

The grandiose mock-Gothic Willersley Castle was built by Richard Arkwright between 1782 and 1788 as his mansion and family home. Unfortunately, he never lived there; the castle was burnt down in 1791 and he died before it was rebuilt and finished. His son, however, lived there, and it later become a Methodist guest house. Some of those guests can be seen on the steps to the left of the picture.

DARLEY DALE
The Church 1892

The parish church of St Helen dates mainly from the 13th and 14th centuries, and is one of the finest in Derbyshire. But its main claim to fame is the massive yew tree which stands in the churchyard and can be seen on the extreme right of this photograph. Its age has been variously estimated at between 600 and 4,000 years, and it was almost certainly there before the church.

◆

GRINDLEFORD
Stoke Hall 1896

Stoke Hall, on the Calver road outside Grindleford, was originally built by Sir William Cavendish, who fought for Charles I at the Battle of Marston Moor in 1644. It was rebuilt in 1757 as the Peakland home of the Earls of Bradford. It is a five-bay two-and-a-half-storey house built in the classical style, complete with Tuscan columns around the door. It later became a hotel and is now in private hands.

DARLEY DALE, THE CHURCH 1892 31305

GRINDLEFORD, STOKE HALL 1896 37826

GRINDLEFORD, THE VILLAGE c1955 G182015
Here we see Main Road, showing the village shop on the right, and the road swinging round to the right to cross Grindleford Bridge over the River Derwent at the bottom of the hill. In the background is the wooded ridge of Yarncliff and Bole Hill, where there was once a lead smelter.

GRINDLEFORD, THE VILLAGE SQUARE c1960 G182031
The War Memorial (right) is based on Eyam's Saxon cross, and stands on what was once the village green and the centre of the village, now on the Hathersage road. Grindleford's Methodist Church on the left of the photograph was built in 1905, replacing an earlier chapel which was visited by John Wesley in 1776.

GRINDLEFORD, GENERAL VIEW C1960 G182036

This view across the Derwent Valley is taken from the Hathersage Road, just outside Grindleford. It looks north towards the prominent gritstone tors of Mother Cap and Over Owler Tor on Hathersage Moor, with the long line of the crags of Stanage Edge in the far distance.

LADYBOWER, THE RESERVOIR C1955 L294005

Here we see the decorative entrance gates to the Ladybower Dam, just outside Bamford, looking towards the white concrete Ashopton Viaduct in the distance, under which are the foundations of what was once the village of Ashopton, on the A57 Snake Road. The reservoir was officially inaugurated in September 1945 by King George VI, who unveiled a memorial tablet and opened the two overflow shafts, one of which is seen to the right.

LADYBOWER, THE RESERVOIR c1955 L294009
A shepherd would not dare to drive his flock along the road alongside the Ladybower Reservoir today, such is the volume of traffic visiting the Upper Derwent Valley. Over the water, the green slopes of Whinstone Lee Tor lead up to the heights of Derwent Edge.

LADYBOWER, THE RESERVOIR c1955 L294002
This view looks south up the northern arm of the Ladybower Reservoir towards the distant hills of Derwent Edge, Bamford Edge and Great Tor, with Crook Hill on the right. The Ladybower Reservoir was constructed during the Second World War to provide water for Sheffield and the East Midland cities of Nottingham, Derby and Leicester.

MATLOCK, THE DALE C1955 M273041

This almost aerial view of the Derwent Gorge at Matlock Bath was probably taken from the heights of Masson Mount above Matlock Bridge. It shows the prominent 300 foot crag of High Tor (left centre) facing the wooded slopes of the Heights of Abraham across the river. The Prospect Tower at Matlock Bath can just be made out peeping above the trees, and the wooded hill in the background is Hagg Wood at Cromford.

MATLOCK, THE TOWN CENTRE C1955 M273005

The town centre of Matlock is now known as Crown Square. This view looks up from the roundabout on the A6 towards Bank Road, where a cable tramway operated from 1893, taking passengers to and from Smedley's Hydropathic Establishment, which now houses the offices of Derbyshire County Council.

MATLOCK BANK
The Footbridge 1886 18611
The notice on the cast iron footbridge across the River Derwent advertised the High Tor
Recreation Grounds, the Fern Cave, Lovers' Walks, and the 'Switzerland View'. Matlock and
Matlock Bath, by this time a popular tourist destination, was known in the tourist brochures as
'Little Switzerland'. The Midland Railway line runs across the river by the viaduct to the left.

MATLOCK BANK, GENERAL VIEW 1886 18614

Eight former hamlets called Matlock make up the present town of Matlock, and as the name suggests, Matlock Bank spreads up the eastern bank of the Derwent. A mill chimney is prominent in the picture to the left, while in the background is Smedley Hydropathic Establishment, providing a popular cure for all sort of ills.

MATLOCK BATH, FROM THE STATION 1886 18590

The pretty Derwentside village of Matlock Bath spreads up the wooded hillside named as the Heights of Abraham after General Wolfe's famous victory against the French at Quebec in 1759. Prominent in the picture is the spire of the parish church of the Holy Trinity.

MATLOCK BATH, NORTH PARADE 1892 31272

This photograph shows the centre of Matlock Bath from the bridge which crosses the River Derwent and leads to the railway station. The hotels on the left and right of the photograph show the importance of tourism to the town even at this early date, and the sign on the road in the centre indicates the way to the Heights, Abraham Prospect Tower (seen on the skyline) and Cavern.

MATLOCK BATH, DERWENT TERRACE 1892 31280

Holidaymakers soak up the sun sitting by the banks of the Derwent in this turn of the 20th century photograph. The elegant spire of the parish church of Holy Trinity, built just 50 years earlier, is obvious on the right.

MATLOCK BATH, THE HEIGHTS OF ABRAHAM c1955 M47007

People gather by the Petrifying Well, outside the Matlock Pavilion. The well and fountain has been used for years to 'petrify' objects placed in it, which are eventually coated with tufa from the lime-rich spring water. In the background, the Prospect Tower at the top of the Heights of Abraham can be seen in the trees - now the upper terminus of the famous cable-car ride.

MATLOCK BATH, THE ROYAL CUMBERLAND CAVERN c1955 M47042

The Royal Cumberland Cavern was one of several public show caves in Matlock Bath during the 1950s, and was well known for its formations of calcite and traces of the work of former lead miners. It is no longer open to the public, although visitors can still go underground at the Great Rutland and Masson Caverns on the Heights of Abraham.

MATLOCK BATH
High Tor 1886

This great, 300-foot sheer wall of limestone formed by the Derwent as it cut its impressive gorge between Matlock and Matlock Bath is known as High Tor. There have been 'Recreation Grounds' on the summit of the Tor for many years, and the view from the top is extensive. Today, the face attracts rock climbers and contains some of the most severe routes in the Peak District.

ROWSLEY
The Bridge and the Peacock Inn 1904

This fine five-arched bridge over the River Derwent has carried traffic for nearly four hundred years. It was built in the early 17th century; in 1925 it was widened from 16 feet to 40 feet to carry the increased traffic on the A6 trunk road between Derby and Manchester. The chimneys of the Peacock Inn can be seen in the background.

MATLOCK BATH, HIGH TOR 1886 18609

ROWSLEY, THE BRIDGE AND THE PEACOCK INN 1904 5216

ROWSLEY

The Peacock Inn 1886 18617

Ponies and traps wait for their passengers outside the
17th-century Peacock Inn, just south of Bakewell on
the Matlock road. The Peacock takes its name from
the coat of arms of the Manners family of nearby
Bakewell, and is a favourite haunt of anglers fishing
on the Derwent and Wye, which meet near the village.

BUXTON

The Crescent 1886 18649

John Carr's magnificent Crescent at Buxton, seen here from The Slopes, was built in 1784 by
the 5th Duke of Devonshire in a bid to rival the elegant spa town of Bath in Somerset. In the
background on the left can be seen the dome of the Great Stables and Riding School, later
to become the Royal Hospital, and the Palace Hotel (right) built just 20 years before this
photograph was taken, when the railway reached Buxton.

BUXTON
The New Baths 1902 48186
The Thermal Baths were still being described as the 'New' Baths in 1902, when this photograph was taken. They were built in 1854 by Henry Currey to a design which matched that of the Natural Baths on the other side of the Crescent, which he had built between 1851 and 1854. Today, they form the Cavendish Shopping Arcade, but the original plunge bath can still be seen. Note the row of bath chairs for patients in the foreground.

BUXTON

The Town Hall 1894 34223

Buxton's elegant Victorian Town Hall was only five years
old when this photograph was taken. Designed by W
Pollard of Manchester, it overlooks The Slopes, where a
series of graded paths were laid out in 1811 by Sir Jeffrey
Wyatville for the benefit and recreation of spa visitors at
the nearby hotels.

BUXTON
The Gardens 1886 18659
It must have been difficult to play tennis in the crinolines and hats
worn by these lady players in this photograph of the Ashwood Park
Gardens. The spectators too appear to be overdressed by modern
standards, in suits, long dresses and hats and using umbrellas to
shelter from the sun.

BUXTON

St Ann's Well 1914 67572

St. Ann's Well is the source of the town's warm mineral spring, which has made it famous as a spa since Roman times. The Pump Room, as it was then known, was built in 1894 as part of the spa treatment. On the other side of the building is the public drinking fountain where people can still sample the warm, blue water.

BUXTON
Spring Gardens 1923 B263001
A busy scene in Spring Gardens, the main shopping
street of Buxton. This street is now pedestrianised.
Note the many signs for cafes along the street and the
awnings across the pavements, which protected the
goods in the shops from fading in the sunlight.

BUXTON, SOLOMON'S TEMPLE 1914 67579
Solomon's Temple, a limestone tower standing on the 1,443ft summit of Grin Low to the south of Buxton, was built in 1896 by local landowner Solomon Mycock, apparently to provide work for the unemployed - a common reason for many follies. It commands extensive views and now stands in the centre of a country park.

BUXTON
The Cat and Fiddle 1894
The Cat and Fiddle Inn, on the Buxton to Macclesfield road, is the second highest public house in England, standing on bleak moorland at the head of the Goyt Valley at 1,690 feet above the sea. Note the pony and trap taking a well-earned rest at the summit, and the two customers taking advantage of a rare sunny spell by having their drinks outside.

BUXTON
The Cat and Fiddle 1914
By 1914, motorised transport had arrived at the Cat and Fiddle, and a fine array of new motor cars and a motor cycle complete with wickerwork sidecar can now be seen outside the airy pub. The proprietor at the time was Joseph Tomlinson, according to the sign on the wall by the carved panel of a cat playing a fiddle, which gave the inn its name.

BUXTON, THE CAT AND FIDDLE 1894 34244

BUXTON, THE CAT AND FIDDLE 1914 67581

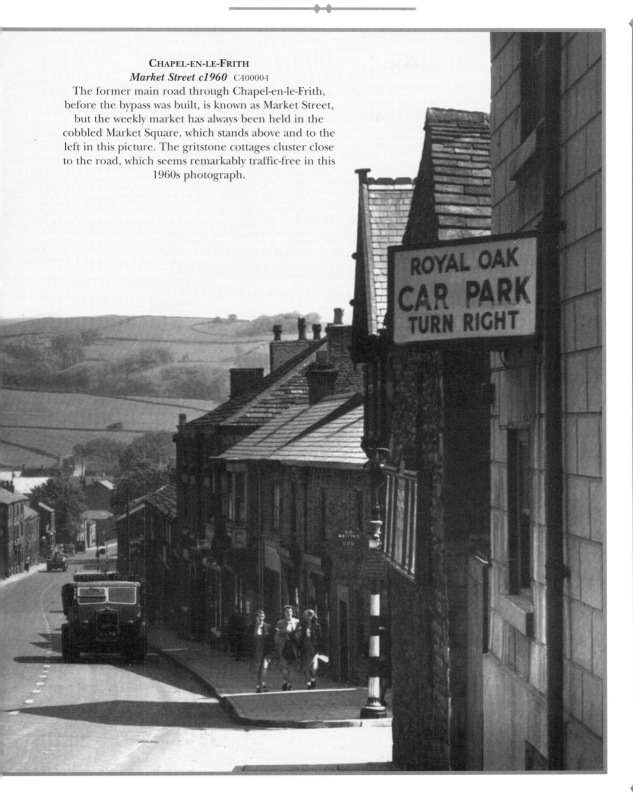

CHAPEL-EN-LE-FRITH
Market Street c1960 C400004
The former main road through Chapel-en-le-Frith,
before the bypass was built, is known as Market Street,
but the weekly market has always been held in the
cobbled Market Square, which stands above and to the
left in this picture. The gritstone cottages cluster close
to the road, which seems remarkably traffic-free in this
1960s photograph.

CHAPEL-EN-LE-FRITH, COMBS RESERVOIR c1960 C400018

Combs Reservoir lies in a depression in the hills to the west of Chapel-en-le-Frith near the villages of Combs and Tunstead Milton. It was built as early as 1794 as a compensating reservoir for the Peak Forest Canal, and is now used by a local sailing club. In the background of this photograph is the escarpment of Ladder Hill, which rises to 1,329 feet and now carries a radio mast.

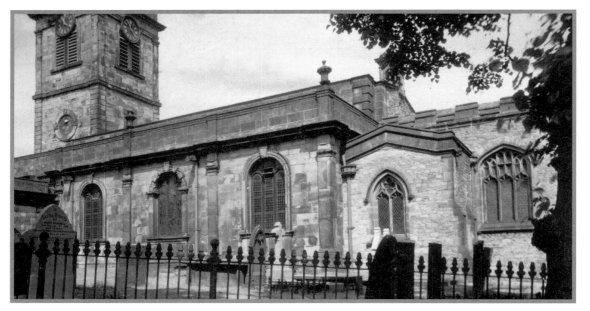

CHAPEL-EN-LE-FRITH, THE PARISH CHURCH c1960 C400001

Chapel's parish church of St Thomas a Becket is an elegant Georgian structure, rebuilt in 1733 by George Platt of Rotherham. Its medieval predecessor was the scene in 1648 of one of the most gruesome episodes in the Peak's history, when 1,500 Scottish soldiers were imprisoned there for two weeks. Forty-eight died in what became known as 'The Black Hole of Derbyshire'.

CHAPEL-EN-LE-FRITH, VIEW ACROSS COMBS c1950 C404005

This view from Combs looks south towards the rocky escarpment of Combs Edge in the background. Note the horned, Shorthorn cattle in the foreground. Once the most popular dairy breed in the Peak, they have now been almost exclusively replaced by the ubiquitous black-and-white Friesians.

HAYFIELD, THE CHURCH c1960 H298001

The fine Georgian tower of the church of St Matthew overlooks the main street of Hayfield. It was rebuilt in 1818, and the chancel was added in 1894. The churchyard was the scene of two supposed 'resurrections' during the 18th century, one at least being caused by the flooding of the River Kinder.

HAYFIELD, MARKET STREET c1960 H298002
A couple of lads chat outside the bank on the street corner of Market Street. This sleepy little Pennine town on the western slopes of Kinder Scout formerly had wool, cotton, papermaking and textile printing mills, all powered by the fast-flowing waters of the Kinder and Sett Rivers.

HAYFIELD, MOUNT FAMINE c1960 H298010
The shapely cone of Mount Famine (1,552ft) is a south-western outlier from Kinder Scout, and overlooks Hayfield to the south. Its name is significant: it was chosen to indicate the poor nature of the soil conditions on the hill, which were thought most likely to result in famine for anyone who farmed them.

HAYFIELD, KINDER VALLEY FROM STUBBS PIECE c1960 H298045
Stubbs Piece takes its name from Stubbs Farm, to the east of Hayfield in the wooded Kinder River Valley; this leads towards the grim heights of Kinder Scout (2,088ft), the highest point in the Peak District, which can be seen in the background. The houses among the trees are on Kinder Road, which leads to the Kinder Reservoir, and is a popular approach to the mountain for walkers.

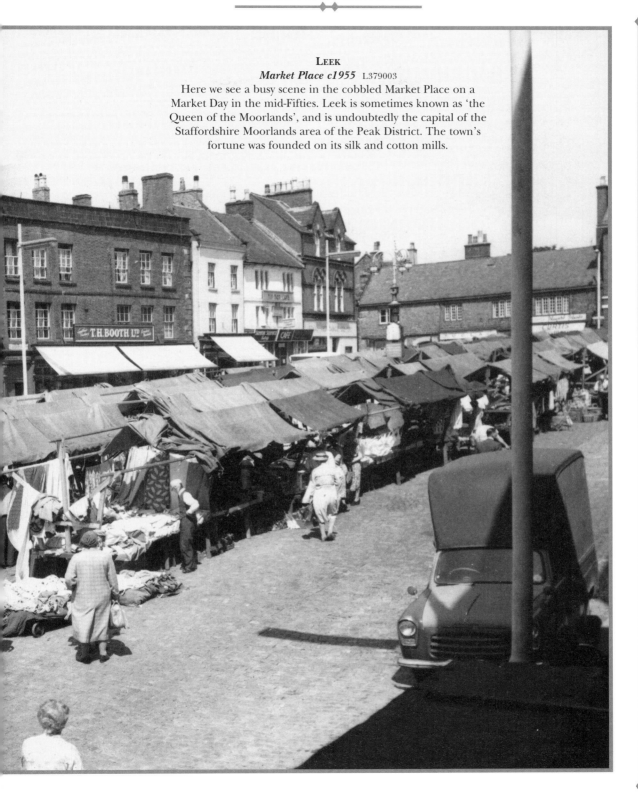

LEEK

Market Place c1955 L379003

Here we see a busy scene in the cobbled Market Place on a Market Day in the mid-Fifties. Leek is sometimes known as 'the Queen of the Moorlands', and is undoubtedly the capital of the Staffordshire Moorlands area of the Peak District. The town's fortune was founded on its silk and cotton mills.

LEEK, DERBY STREET c1955 L379004

This is an early traffic roundabout at the junction of the A53 Buxton to Stoke-on-Trent road with the A523 Macclesfield road. It is interesting to note that Stoke-on-Trent is not mentioned in the road sign, which merely states 'Potteries'.

LEEK, THE NICHOLSON WAR MEMORIAL c1955 L379006

The grand white marble clock tower of the Nicholson War Memorial dominates this view of Leek town centre. It is more correctly known as a peace memorial, and was raised by Sir Arthur Nicholson in memory of his own son and all the other sons of Leek who died during the First World War.

LEEK, ST EDWARD STREET c1955 L379009

This is the junction of St Edward Street and Brook Street, framed by the then-fashionable mock-Tudor fronted shops. St Edward Street takes its name from the dedication of the town's mother church to St Edward. It is a fine building, with a pinnacled 14th-century tower.

RAINOW, MACCLESFIELD ROAD c1965 R307003

The A537 Buxton-Macclesfield moorland road drops down towards the Cheshire Plain near the hilltop village of Rainow, on the western side of the Peak District. Only two cars are seen on the lonely road in this photograph.

RAINOW, THE RISING SUN c1965 R307004

The Rising Sun at Rainow, on the left of this photograph, sold Hovis teas as well as Smith's Macclesfield ales to passing ramblers in the 1960s. The row of gritstone cottages opposite, with stone-flagged pavements and gritstone slab roofs, are typical of west Pennine villages.

RUDYARD, THE LAKE c1955 R350026

Rudyard Lake, three miles north of Leek, was also built as a compensating reservoir, this time for the Caldon Canal, in 1799. It was a popular Victorian resort, with regular trains running on the North Staffordshire Railway from Leek on Bank Holidays. But it is perhaps best known for providing the name of the writer Rudyard Kipling, whose mother and father became engaged there.

TINTWISTLE, OLD ROAD c1960 T204029
Tintwistle - locally pronounced 'Tinsel' - stands at the entrance to Longdendale in the far north-west of the Peak District. This view of Old Road shows typical Pennine gritstone terraces lining the street, which leads into the wilds of the Longdendale-Woodhead cross-Pennine route.

WILDBOARCLOUGH, ST SAVIOUR'S PARISH CHURCH c1960 W369002
The squat sandstone building of St Saviour's parish church is surrounded by rhododendrons in this secluded valley on the western edge of the Peak District. Said to be the last place in England where a wild boar was killed, Wildboarclough shelters under the shapely cone of Shutlingsloe, one of the only true 'peaks' in the Peak District.

WILDBOARCLOUGH, THE POST OFFICE c1960 W369004
For many years this fine 18th-century building was the largest village post office in the country. Built as the office block for Crag Mill, a silk mill which later provided carpets for the Great Exhibition of 1851, the building later served partly as a post office and more recently was converted for residential use.

WILDBOARCLOUGH, CRAG BRIDGE c1960 W369008
The name of this bridge over the Clough Brook gives away the ancient name of the village now known as Wildboarclough. It used to be called Crag, and there is still a Crag Hall and a Crag Inn in the village. It was the Clough Brook which provided the power for Wildboarclough's silk mill.

WILDBOARCLOUGH, CRAG HALL AND SHUTLINGSLOE c1960 W369011
The gable-like ridge of Shutlingsloe, whose summit is 1,659ft above the sea, dominates almost every view of Wildboarclough. It commands tremendous views across the Cheshire Plain and into the hills of the Peak. In the centre foreground, behind the trees, is Crag Hall, which takes its name from the old name of the village.

WILDBOARCLOUGH, THREE SHIRES BRIDGE c1960 W369301

Three Shires Bridge is an idyllic spot sheltered in the moorlands to the east of Wildboarclough. This old packhorse bridge takes its name from being on the junction of the borders of Cheshire, Derbyshire and Staffordshire, and was once the scene of illegal prize-fighting, where contestants could easily avoid arrest by nipping across the county boundary when approached by the law.

WINCLE, THE ROACHES c1955 W416024

The jagged gritstone towers of The Roaches always present a startling sight for travellers approaching the Peak District on the A53 Leek-Buxton road. This view actually shows Hen Cloud, a 1,345ft outlier from the main ridge of The Roaches, which can be seen in the background to the left. Rock climbers like Joe Brown and Don Whillans were just starting to explore the hardest routes on these steep faces when this picture was taken in the mid-Fifties.

Index

Alport 26

Alstonefield 16

Ashbourne 16, 17

Ashford-in-the-Water 26, 27, 28

Bakewell 29, 30-31, 32-33, 34, 35

Bamford 70

Baslow 70, 71

Bonsall 18

Bradwell 56, 57, 58, 59

Buxton 88–89, 90, 91, 92–93, 94–95, 96–97, 98, 99

Calver 72, 73

Castleton 59, 60–61, 62, 63

Chapel-en-le-firth 100–101, 102, 103

Chelmonton 36

Cromford 74

Darley Dale 75

Dovedale 18, 19, 20, 21

Edensor 37

Eyam 37, 38

Great Hucklow 64

Great Longstone 39, 40

Grindleford 75, 76, 77

Haddon Hall 40, 41, 42

Hartington 22

Hathersage 65, 66–67, 68, 69

Hayfield 103, 104, 105

Hope 69

Ilam 23

Ladybower 77, 78

Leek 107, 108, 109

Mappleton 23, 24

Matlock 79,

Matlock Bank 80–81, 82

Matlock Bath 82, 83, 84, 85

Millers Dale 43

Monsal Dale 44–45, 46

Over Haddon 47

Rainow 109, 110

Rowsley 85, 86–87

Rudyard 110

Stoney Middleton 48, 49, 50, 51

Thorpe 24

Tideswell 51, 52

Tintwistle 111

Wildboarclough 112, 113, 114

Wincle 114

Winster 53, 54

Wirksworth 25

Youlgreave 55

Frith Book Co Titles

Frith Book Company publish over a 100 new titles each year. For latest catalogue please contact Frith Book Co.

Town Books 96pp, 100 photos. County and Themed Books 128pp, 150 photos
(unless specified) All titles hardback laminated case and jacket
except those indicated pb (paperback)

Around Barnstaple	1-85937-084-5	£12.99
Around Blackpool	1-85937-049-7	£12.99
Around Bognor Regis	1-85937-055-1	£12.99
Around Bristol	1-85937-050-0	£12.99
Around Cambridge	1-85937-092-6	£12.99
Cheshire	1-85937-045-4	£14.99
Around Chester	1-85937-090-X	£12.99
Around Chesterfield	1-85937-071-3	£12.99
Around Chichester	1-85937-089-6	£12.99
Cornwall	1-85937-054-3	£14.99
Cotswolds	1-85937-099-3	£14.99
Around Derby	1-85937-046-2	£12.99
Devon	1-85937-052-7	£14.99
Dorset	1-85937-075-6	£14.99
Dorset Coast	1-85937-062-4	£14.99
Around Dublin	1-85937-058-6	£12.99
East Anglia	1-85937-059-4	£14.99
Around Eastbourne	1-85937-061-6	£12.99
English Castles	1-85937-078-0	£14.99
Around Falmouth	1-85937-066-7	£12.99
Hampshire	1-85937-064-0	£14.99
Isle of Man	1-85937-065-9	£14.99
Around Maidstone	1-85937-056-X	£12.99
North Yorkshire	1-85937-048-9	£14.99
Around Nottingham	1-85937-060-8	£12.99
Around Penzance	1-85937-069-1	£12.99
Around Reading	1-85937-087-X	£12.99
Around St Ives	1-85937-068-3	£12.99
Around Salisbury	1-85937-091-8	£12.99
Around Scarborough	1-85937-104-3	£12.99
Scottish Castles	1-85937-077-2	£14.99
Around Sevenoaks and Tonbridge	1-85937-057-8	£12.99

Sheffield and S Yorkshire	1-85937-070-5		£14.99
Shropshire	1-85937-083-7		£14.99
Staffordshire	1-85937-047-0	(96pp)	£12.99
Suffolk	1-85937-074-8		£14.99
Surrey	1-85937-081-0		£14.99
Around Torbay	1-85937-063-2		£12.99
Wiltshire	1-85937-053-5		£14.99
Around Bakewell	1-85937-113-2		£12.99
Around Bournemouth	1-85937-067-5		£12.99
Cambridgeshire	1-85937-086-1		£14.99
Essex	1-85937-082-9		£14.99
Around Great Yarmouth	1-85937-085-3		£12.99
Hertfordshire	1-85937-079-9		£14.99
Isle of Wight	1-85937-114-0		£14.99
Around Lincoln	1-85937-111-6		£12.99
Oxfordshire	1-85937-076-4		£14.99
Around Shrewsbury	1-85937-110-8		£12.99
South Devon Coast	1-85937-107-8		£14.99
Around Stratford upon Avon	1-85937-098-5		£12.99
West Midlands	1-85937-109-4		£14.99

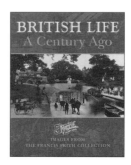

British Life A Century Ago
246 x 189mm
144pp, hardback.
Black and white
Lavishly illustrated with photos
from the turn of the century,
and with extensive commentary.
It offers a unique insight into
the social history and heritage
of bygone Britain.

1-85937-103-5 £17.99

Available from your local bookshop or from the publisher

Around Bath	1-85937-097-7	£12.99	Mar
Cumbria	1-85937-101-9	£14.99	Mar
Down the Thames	1-85937-121-3	£14.99	Mar
Around Exeter	1-85937-126-4	£12.99	Mar
Greater Manchester	1-85937-108-6	£14.99	Mar
Around Harrogate	1-85937-112-4	£12.99	Mar
Around Leicester	1-85937-073-x	£12.99	Mar
Around Liverpool	1-85937-051-9	£12.99	Mar
Northumberland and Tyne & Wear			
	1-85937-072-1	£14.99	Mar
Around Oxford	1-85937-096-9	£12.99	Mar
Around Plymouth	1-85937-119-1	£12.99	Mar
Around Southport	1-85937-106-x	£12.99	Mar
Welsh Castles	1-85937-120-5	£14.99	Mar
Canals and Waterways	1-85937-129-9	£17.99	Apr
Around Guildford	1-85937-117-5	£12.99	Apr
Around Horsham	1-85937-127-2	£12.99	Apr
Around Ipswich	1-85937-133-7	£12.99	Apr
Ireland (pb)	1-85937-181-7	£9.99	Apr
London (pb)	1-85937-183-3	£9.99	Apr
New Forest	1-85937-128-0	£14.99	Apr
Around Newark	1-85937-105-1	£12.99	Apr
Around Newquay	1-85937-140-x	£12.99	Apr
Scotland (pb)	1-85937-182-5	£9.99	Apr
Around Southampton	1-85937-088-8	£12.99	Apr
Sussex (pb)	1-85937-184-1	£9.99	Apr
Around Winchester	1-85937-139-6	£12.99	Apr
Around Belfast	1-85937-094-2	£12.99	May
Colchester (pb)	1-85937-188-4	£8.99	May
Exmoor	1-85937-132-9	£14.99	May
Leicestershire (pb)	1-85937-185-x	£9.99	May
Lincolnshire	1-85937-135-3	£14.99	May
North Devon Coast	1-85937-146-9	£14.99	May
Nottinghamshire (pb)	1-85937-187-6	£9.99	May
Peak District	1-85937-100-0	£14.99	May
Around Truro	1-85937-147-7	£12.99	May
Yorkshire (pb)	1-85937-186-8	£9.99	May

Berkshire (pb)	1-85937-191-4	£9.99	Jun
Brighton (pb)	1-85937-192-2	£8.99	Jun
County Durham	1-85937-123-x	£14.99	Jun
Dartmoor	1-85937-145-0	£14.99	Jun
Down the Severn	1-85937-118-3	£14.99	Jun
East London	1-85937-080-2	£14.99	Jun
East Sussex	1-85937-130-2	£14.99	Jun
Glasgow (pb)	1-85937-190-6	£8.99	Jun
Kent (pb)	1-85937-189-2	£9.99	Jun
Kent Living Memories	1-85937-125-6	£14.99	Jun
Redhill to Reigate	1-85937-137-x	£12.99	Jun
Stone Circles & Ancient Monuments			
	1-85937-143-4	£17.99	Jun
Victorian & Edwardian Kent			
	1-85937-149-3	£14.99	Jun
Victorian & Edwardian Maritime Album			
	1-85937-144-2	£17.99	Jun
Victorian & Edwardian Yorkshire			
	1-85937-154-x	£14.99	Jun
West Sussex	1-85937-148-5	£14.99	Jun
Churches of Berkshire	1-85937-170-1	£17.99	Jul
Churches of Dorset	1-85937-172-8	£17.99	Jul
Derbyshire (pb)	1-85937-196-5	£9.99	Jul
Edinburgh (pb)	1-85937-193-0	£8.99	Jul
Folkstone	1-85937-124-8	£12.99	Jul
Gloucestershire	1-85937-102-7	£14.99	Jul
Herefordshire	1-85937-174-4	£14.99	Jul
North London	1-85937-206-6	£14.99	Jul
Norwich (pb)	1-85937-194-9	£8.99	Jul
Ports and Harbours	1-85937-208-2	£17.99	Jul
Somerset and Avon	1-85937-153-1	£14.99	Jul
South Devon Living Memories			
	1-85937-168-x	£14.99	Jul
Warwickshire (pb)	1-85937-203-1	£9.99	Jul
Worcestershire	1-85937-152-3	£14.99	Jul
Yorkshire Living Memories			
	1-85937-166-3	£14.99	Jul

FRITH PRODUCTS & SERVICES

Francis Frith would doubtless be pleased to know that the pioneering publishing venture he started in 1860 still continues today. More than a hundred and thirty years later, The Francis Frith Collection continues in the same innovative tradition and is now one of the foremost publishers of vintage photographs in the world. Some of the current activities include:

Interior Decoration

Today Frith's photographs can be seen framed and as giant wall murals in thousands of pubs, restaurants, hotels, banks, retail stores and other public buildings throughout the country. In every case they enhance the unique local atmosphere of the places they depict and provide reminders of gentler days in an increasingly busy and frenetic world.

Product Promotions

Frith products have been used by many major companies to promote the sales of their own products or to reinforce their own history and heritage. Brands include Hovis bread, Courage beers, Scots Porage Oats, Colman's mustard, Cadbury's foods, Mellow Birds coffee, Dunhill pipe tobacco, Guinness, and Bulmer's Cider.

Genealogy and Family History

As the interest in family history and roots grows world-wide, more and more people are turning to Frith's photographs of Great Britain for images of the towns, villages and streets where their ancestors lived; and, of course, photographs of the churches and chapels where their ancestors were christened, married and buried are an essential part of every genealogy tree and family album.

A series of easy-to-use CD Roms is planned for publication, and an increasing number of Frith photographs will be able to be viewed on specialist genealogy sites. A growing range of Frith books will be available on CD.

The Internet

Already thousands of Frith photographs can be viewed and purchased on the internet. By the end of the year 2000 some 60,000 Frith photographs will be available on the internet. The number of sites is constantly expanding, each focussing on different products and services from the Collection.
Some of the sites are listed below.

www.townpages.co.uk
www.icollector.com
www.barclaysquare.co.uk
www.cornwall-online.co.uk

For background information on the Collection look at the three following sites:

www.francisfrith.com
www.francisfrith.co.uk
www.frithbook.co.uk

Frith Products

All Frith photographs are available Framed or just as Mounted Prints, and can be ordered from the address below. From time to time other products - Address Books, Calendars, Table Mats, etc - are available.

> **For further information:**
> if you would like further information on any of the above aspects of the Frith business please contact us at the address below:
> **The Francis Frith Collection,**
> **Frith's Barn, Teffont, Salisbury, Wiltshire,**
> **England SP3 5QP.**
> Tel: +44 (0)1722 716 376 Fax: +44 (0)1722 716 881   Email: uksales@francisfrith.com

To receive your FREE Mounted Print

Mounted Print
Overall size 14 x 11 inches

Cut out this Voucher and return it with your remittance for £1.50 to cover postage and handling. Choose any photograph included in this book. Your SEPIA print will be A4 in size, and mounted in a cream mount with burgundy rule lines, overall size 14 x 11 inches.

Order additional Mounted Prints at HALF PRICE (only £7.49 each*)

If there are further pictures you would like to order, possibly as gifts for friends and family, acquire them at half price (no additional postage and handling required).

Have your Mounted Prints framed*

For an additional £14.95 per print you can have your chosen Mounted Print framed in an elegant polished wood and gilt moulding, overall size 16 x 13 inches (no additional postage and handling required).

---

* IMPORTANT!
These special prices are only available if ordered using the original voucher on this page (no copies permitted) and at the same time as your free Mounted Print, for delivery to the same address

---

Frith Collectors' Guild

From time to time we publish a magazine of news and stories about Frith photographs and further special offers of Frith products. If you would like 12 months FREE membership, please return this form.

Send completed forms to:
The Francis Frith Collection, Frith's Barn, Teffont, Salisbury, Wiltshire SP3 5QP

Voucher for FREE and Reduced Price Frith Prints

Picture no.	Page number	Qty	Mounted @ £7.49	Framed + £14.95	Total Cost
		1	**Free of charge***	£	£
			£7.49	£	£
			£7.49	£	£
			£7.49	£	£
			£7.49	£	£
			£7.49	£	£
			* Post & handling		£1.50

Book Title . . . .   **Total Order Cost** | **£** |

Please do not photocopy this voucher. Only the original is valid, so please cut it out and return it to us.

I enclose a cheque / postal order for £ . . . .
made payable to 'The Francis Frith Collection'
OR please debit my Mastercard / Visa / Switch / Amex card

Number . . . .

Expires . . . . Signature . . . .

Name Mr/Mrs/Ms . . . .

Address . . . .

. . . .

. . . .

. . . .

. . . . Postcode . . . .

Daytime Tel No . . . .   Valid to 31/12/01

The Francis Frith Collectors' Guild

Please enrol me as a member for 12 months free of charge.

Name Mr/Mrs/Ms . . . .

Address . . . .

. . . .

. . . .

. . . . Postcode . . . .

Free Print - see overleaf